ADHD Kids;Guide For Parents(Successful Parenting) And Teachers

Susan Myer

Table Of Contents

Chapter 1

Overview of ADHD

A total of 6.1 million youngsters in the US suffer from attention deficit hyperactivity disorder (ADHD). Organization, ADHD youngsters struggle with following directions, impulse control, and other daily abilities. Although these actions would seem to show that a youngster is acting rebelliously or inappropriately, this is not the case. These tasks are noticeably more difficult for children with ADHD to complete than for children without ADHD. Children with ADHD struggle with executive function skills. The life skills required for this include, but are not limited to, planning, patience, self-control, maintaining concentration on a goal, and emotion regulation. It's vital to bear in mind that some children with ADHD lack the perspective or mental capacity to understand how other people view their actions and behaviors. Children with ADHD who struggle with executive function may need special attention at home and in the classroom.

Most often, kids with ADHD aren't able to comprehend how they come across when dealing with others. They try their hardest, yet they still have trouble tuning in and "walking in the other person's shoes." A child with ADHD may accidentally forget social norms and come across as impolite and uncaring when they are bored, anxious, hungry, fatigued, or having trouble controlling their emotions.

Children with ADHD may find it difficult to read social cues, but with the correct help, they may work on extending their viewpoint, putting themselves in another person's shoes, and regulating their behavior to live up to expectations.

No matter how hard they try, your child will usually require assistance and support if they are to change. It won't take place instantly.Behavior that resembles an iceberg is shown by a youngster with ADHD. How a youngster act is determined by the invisible component. To be able to assist your child in acquiring the abilities that promote growth and transformation, you must first understand those deeper dimensions. Kids occasionally grow restless in class or have trouble waiting for their turn, and this is perfectly normal. In children with ADHD, these habits are enduring. They occur regularly and prevent the child from succeeding at home or in school.

A child with ADHD could have trouble finishing their homework, keeping their room tidy, making friends, and paying attention to adults. This may make an ADHD child more irritable and make their symptoms worse.

Children with ADHD can be friendly, but their impulsivity can cause problems and regularly alienates others, including their siblings, instructors, and classmates. They don't wait for their turn, interrupt others, get angry easily, take risks, and their emotions might bubble over like water at a rolling boil: They might be huffy, lash out angrily, or have temper tantrums. All of this at playgrounds and in classrooms comes with enormous societal costs.

They are not well-organized, prone to forgetting things, and prone to procrastinate. They struggle to put up the time and effort required to complete a task, especially if it entails completing a school project on a topic they don't find appealing.

Incidental learning, or the process of learning by accident, is difficult for Adhd youngsters to do. It might require a lot of practice for them to learn the rules. Both disorders can cause issues since it requires a lot of work to regulate impulsivity. Hyperactive kids might not be as driven to follow the rules. Inattentive kids would be and can cause problems because they might frequently forget the rules.

Young children are often lively, noisy, and prone to impulsive conduct. In addition to climbing and running, they like to play loudly and noisily. They move around a lot and fidget, and they like going outside to see the world around them. Kids frequently experience difficulties with listening, remembering details, and adhering to directions. This entire situation is typical of being a kid. Overwhelmed and frustrated feelings are quite common in children with ADHD. They struggle with executive function and have a hard time managing their emotions. They might have a lot of difficulty with, for instance:

- Planning and prioritizing
- The ability to focus and remember information.

School can be Difficult

Children with ADHD usually experience numerous difficulties in school. They misplace books, overlook homework, carry messy bags, and struggle to remember test dates. For children who are not paying attention, being attentive in class can be very challenging. They could frequently get into problems in class for fidgeting or acting up.

Chapter 2

How to Manage your Emotions as a Parent
Stop the Yelling, be Calm and
Compassionate

The secret to controlling emotions is having the inner fortitude to restrain our intensely powerful feelings. This occasionally necessitates an internal pep talk, especially if your children are depending on you.

By managing our behavior, we can overcome obstacles such as returning to normal after a loss, calming down after anger, or finding comfort in ourselves after a major failure.

However, there is a stronger incentive to restrain your emotions when our kids are around. By demonstrating how to respond in moments of discomfort, fear, anger, sadness, and grief, parents help their kids learn how to face challenging circumstances. We have the opportunity to set a positive example for our children during these challenging times.

Controlling one's emotions is among the most crucial life skills. Although humans have a vast variety of personalities and temperaments, parents are still only human. While some parents are calm and collected, others are more likely to lose it or cry. To feel those feelings without losing control may be difficult. It can be helpful to pause and contemplate the kind of example you are providing when coping with difficult emotions. Parents will later serve as role models for their children's behavior.

To teach their children how to self-regulate, parents must model calm behavior. Parents frequently respond with the same ferocity their children are displaying, but this only makes things worse.

However, it's crucial to recognize and control these emotions since it's how you respond in these circumstances that determine how well your child will turn out. His ability to develop effective coping mechanisms and his future behavior are both influenced by your response.

Anger and frustration-based reactions are more likely to make the youngster feel worse than to promote relaxation and coping. One of the most crucial ways you can lessen both your own and your child's distress is by learning to control your reactions.
Additionally, it teaches kids how to control their own emotions, a life skill that will improve their academic performance as well as their ability to form friendships and other relationships as they mature. It is undoubtedly much simpler to say than to accomplish to control powerful negative feelings. However, the work is worthwhile because you and your child will benefit greatly from it.

Pay Attention to your Emotions

There is no right or incorrect way to feel.

Your actions will determine whether your feelings are constructive or destructive. The most crucial thing is to become aware of and take responsibility for your emotions so that you can consciously choose how to react. Consider your child's actions in light of their temperament and developmental stage.

It's important to set realistic expectations since they affect how you handle your own emotions and responses to your child's current behavior. If you see the action as manipulative or as intentional harm (such as biting or punching), you are more likely to respond in a way that agitates rather than soothes your child.

Furthermore, irrational outbursts rarely teach students effective coping mechanisms. Instead, if you understand that these actions are part of a child's normal growth, you will be far more likely to approach your child with empathy and respond to them in a way that is both composed and effective.

As a parent, you are aware of how easily your feelings can sometimes take control. The buttons you didn't know you possessed can be pushed by kids.

Being a parent might be frustrating, but you're not the only one who does it. The good news is that you may modify your communication style with your children so that you no longer yell at them in monologues but instead engage them in respectful discussion.

Executive function, or the capacity to plan, organize, restrain impulses, and finish tasks, is typically impaired in children with ADHD. As a result, you will need to assume the role of the executive and provide your child with additional direction while they eventually develop their executive abilities.

It's critical to keep in mind that a youngster who ignores, irritates, or embarrasses you isn't intentionally acting in such a way. Children with ADHD desire to sit quietly, maintain a clean and orderly environment in their rooms, and carry out all of their parent's instructions, but they lack the skills to do so.

It will be much simpler to react positively and supportively if you bear in mind that your child's ADHD is just as frustrating for them. You can handle childhood ADHD while having a stable, happy home if you have patience, compassion, and lots of support.

Spanking should never be used to discipline a child who has attention deficit hyperactivity disorder (ADHD) since the physical act of spanking might cause emotional harm.

Why Do Parents Shout?

The quickest response is that we raise our voices when we are stressed or furious. However, it is rare for such to be the answer. For a brief period, it might calm the kids and make them submissive, but it won't change their attitudes or conduct. It trains kids to fear you rather than to grasp the effects of their actions, to put it simply. To learn, children look to their parents.

A child's behavior will match what they believe to be "normal" in their family if they witness anger and the accompanying aggression like shouting.
The same applies to your kids. Since raising your voice lowers their receptivity each time, shouting will cause kids to tune you out and make discipline more difficult.
Children become more violent when they are yelled at, both physically and verbally. Any time someone yells, regardless of the situation, they are expressing fury. Children are frightened and uneasy as a result.
Yelling is a horrible way to teach your youngster how to control his emotions. Parents frequently believe that their voice volume will have a greater impact on their child, however, this is untrue. The child only

hears the fury. The incident quickly gets out of hand.

It's very normal to occasionally feel furious with your child. It's inappropriate to yell at her nonstop. You know you can control your anger if necessary since you wouldn't consider yelling and swearing at friends or coworkers.

Alternatives to Speaking Louder

It is simpler to discipline kids who have a close emotional bond with their parents. Children will be more responsive to talk and listen before a quarrel turns into an irate yelling episode if they feel secure and unwaveringly loved.

Here's a method for positive discipline that doesn't entail yelling.

Take a Break.

Before you lose control and raise your voice out of anger, try to stop yourself. You allow yourself to reevaluate and take deep breaths, which will help you calm down, by moving away from the area of dispute for a short while.

It also teaches your kids how to set boundaries and healthily deal with intense emotions.

Discuss Your Feelings

You may teach your kids about the range of human emotions by expressing them all, from happiness and excitement to sadness, rage, jealousy, and frustration.

Encourage your kids to do the same by talking about your feelings. They will learn to respect themselves and others and build wholesome connections as a result.

Address Inappropriate Behavior Strongly but Calmly.

Sometimes kids act badly. That's a necessary component of maturation. Talk to them firmly while maintaining their dignity and making it plain that certain behaviors are not acceptable.

Instead of speaking to them from above or from a distance, get down to their eye level. Recognize mutual problem-solving and courteous conduct at the same time.

A Word About Necessities

Children are happier and behave better overall when their basic needs, such as sleep and hunger, are satisfied. Creating routines will also help children feel less nervous and lower their likelihood of misbehaving.

How to Handle Yelling

Despite your best efforts to avoid yelling, you may nevertheless occasionally shout. I understand. Your kids will learn a valuable lesson if you own up to it and apologize: Everyone makes errors, and you should always say you're sorry.

If your kids shout, tell them that this is not the appropriate way to communicate and that there are boundaries. They must be aware that you would listen to them as long as they are respectful.

When you are angry or stressed, set an example for your kids by giving yourself some time to collect yourself before speaking to them.

They will learn habits that will help them manage conflict more effectively throughout their lives. By doing so, you will be able to educate your kids on how to forgive others for their faults as well as their own, and how it promotes good family communication.

If your method of child discipline has included yelling thus far, you are probably already feeling the effects

There's a chance that your kids will yell at each other to communicate.

Instead of speaking politely, they converse back at you and sometimes yell.

To the extent that you are unable to communicate with them healthily, your relationship with them is unstable and turbulent.

They could distance themselves from you and start to take more cues from their friends than you do.

Everything is modifiable. Talk openly with your kids about why screaming is improper and why it is unhealthy to express your anger in this way.

Create a peaceful atmosphere in your home where individuals may converse respectfully and recognize one another's emotions without placing blame, humiliating one another, or passing judgment.

Never give up if you make mistakes. Although it's not an easy journey, it's worthwhile. Recognizing that you have a problem is the first step in learning how to deal with it if your anger frequently spills over onto your kids and you struggle to control your temper regularly.

By doing this, you'll feel better about yourself and be able to talk to your kids in a kind and peaceful manner.

On the other side, calmness is reassuring, which lets kids feel loved and accepted despite misbehavior. Don't let your child's behavior bother you. Do not include your feelings over your child's behavior. Even if you don't think their emotions or behavior are appropriate, instead, express empathy and support their sentiments. Provide information in a cool, steady voice.

Instead of shouting or making threats or insults, the goal is to employ a firm yet compassionate tone of voice and word choice. A lot of the time, I advise parents to disguise their displeasure as puzzlement or curiosity: "Oh no, not again. What do you think caused this situation? " or "I'm perplexed by your actions because this is not how I view you."

Make sure your child has the opportunity to witness you supporting others. Bear in mind that deeds speak louder than words. More effectively than any lecture, you can teach your child generosity and responsibility by saying, "I'm going to help grandma fix her garden," or "Your aunt needs my help moving some boxes today." Allow your child to assist in box packing if you are giving away outgrown clothing and toys to less fortunate families.

Keeping your cool under pressure requires effort and time, but it is a true gift. Parenting a child with ADHD can be extremely stressful without having to deal with constant conflict and yelling. The more relaxed you are, the more relaxed they are likely to be, and vice versa. Children with ADHD are also very perceptive. You both gain from maintaining a positive attitude.

You can start down the path of calm parenting by really, truly understanding the causes behind your child's undesired behaviors. Being able to remain calm while you are angry with your child will make you a much better parent. When you notice that you are starting to feel upset or frustrated, use some simple soothing practices.

Be Compassionate

Chapter 3

How you can help your kid with ADHD and help yourself as a parent

The care of a child who suffers from attention deficit hyperactivity disorder (ADHD) can be difficult. Activities of daily living can become demanding and stressful due to the impulsive, fearless, and chaotic behaviors typical of Adhd.
The fact that a child with Adhd is unable to control their behavior must always be kept in mind, even though it can be challenging at times. Since it can be difficult for people with Adhd to control their impulses, they might not think things through or consider the effects of their actions before acting.

Children with ADHD are more easily distracted, impulsive, and hyperactive than children of similar age would be. The ability to control their attention behavior, emotions and activity is more difficult for children with ADHD to learn. Because of this, they frequently exhibit behavior that is challenging for parents to control. Children with ADHD for instance, may exhibit poor effort in their schoolwork, appear disorganized, seem distracted, have trouble listening, trouble Mmto pay attention, need frequent reminders, and struggle with organization.

Children with ADHD who exhibit excessive agitation may:

- When playing, they fidget and seem unable to sit still, climb, jump, or roughhouse, rush instead of taking their time, make careless mistakes, or are constantly on the move (constantly in motion) Children with Adhd may:
- Interrupt frequently and blurt things out
- Do things without thinking that they shouldn't, despite knowing better,
- Possess emotional outbursts, lose their temper, or exhibit a lack of self-control and have difficulty waiting, taking turns, or sharing.

At first, parents might not be aware that these behaviors are symptoms of ADHD. It might appear that a child is simply acting inappropriately. Adhd can make parents feel stressed, impatient, or disrespected.

Because of how their child is acting, parents might feel ashamed. They might question whether or not they contributed to the problem. However, children with Adhd struggle with these abilities because they are not born with them.
Parents who are knowledgeable about Adhd and the most effective parenting strategies can support their children's growth and academic success.

How Can Parents Help?

Many parents think that finding a medication is the only way to treat their child's ADHD. Parents may feel anxious when considering starting their child on medication at a young age. Parents' reactions can improve or worsen ADHD.

Be aware of how ADHD may affect your child. Each child is unique. Determine the issues that your child's ADHD is causing. Some children need to practice listening and paying attention. People need to slow down more often.

One thing at a time, pay attention to teaching your child. Avoid attempting to complete everything at once. Begin modestly. Focus on just one thing. Get involved with your child's school. Speak to your kid's teacher.

Clearly Define Your Expectations

Talk with your child about how you want them to behave before you go somewhere. Instead of responding to what your child does or does not do, put more effort into teaching them what to do. Talk about it. Do not be afraid to discuss ADHD with your child. Help children realize that having

ADHD is not their fault and that they can learn how to reduce the issues it causes.

Spend quality time with one another every day. Even if it's just for a short while, make time to talk and engage in enjoyable activities with your child. Give your child your undivided attention. laud admirable actions. Don't give your child excessive praise, but do let them know when they do something right. Say something like, "You're taking turns so nicely," to your child when they wait their turn.

The most important thing is your relationship with your child. Children with ADHD frequently believe they are failing others, acting improperly, or otherwise not being "good." Be patient, understanding, and accepting to preserve your child's self-esteem. Let your child know that you appreciate all of their positive qualities and that you believe in them. Maintain a loving and positive relationship with your child to build resilience.

Maintain a positive attitude and good physical health.

You, as a parent, lay the foundation for your child's mental and physical well-being. Many of the elements that can have a positive impact on your child's disorder symptoms are under your control.

Maintain a Positive Outlook.

Your optimistic outlook and sound judgment are your best resources for assisting your child in overcoming the challenges of ADHD. You are more likely to be able to connect with your child and encourage him or her to be calm and focused when you are both focused and at ease.

Maintain perspective. Keep in mind that your child's behavior is indicative of a disorder. Most of the time, it is not on purpose. Do not lose your sense of humor. What's embarrassing right now might be humorous tomorrow.

Be willing to make some compromises and don't worry too much about the little things. When your child has finished the day's homework in addition to two other chores, one task left undone is not a big deal. A perfectionist parent will not only be unsatisfied all the time but will also set unrealistic expectations for their ADHD child.

Don't Lose Faith in your Kid

Make a mental list of all the wonderful, priceless, and distinctive qualities your child possesses, or write them down. Have faith in your kid's capacity for growth, learning, and success. As you make your coffee or brush your teeth each day, remind yourself of this.

.

Self-Care

You must lead a healthy lifestyle because you are your child's biggest inspiration and source of strength. You run the risk of overlooking the structure and support you have painstakingly put in place for your child with ADHD if you are overtired or have simply run out of patience.

Be Sure to Rest

Although it's great when friends and family offer to watch your child, you might feel bad about leaving them with an ADHD child or a volunteer. When they offer to help you again take them up on it and talk openly about how to handle your child.

Keep Yourself Healthy

Find healthy eating and exercise routines as well as stress-reduction techniques, such as morning meditation or taking a bath every night. Recognize your illness if you do.
Organize your work and follow a plan
Tasks that occur in predictable patterns and locations are more likely to be completed successfully by children with ADHD. It is

your responsibility to establish and maintain order in your home so that your child understands what to expect from you and what is expected of them.

Enroll your kid in music, art, or sports. Plan easy activities at home to keep your child occupied. These can be activities like playing a game of checkers with your sibling, helping you cook, or drawing a picture. Be careful not to spend too much time playing video games or watching television. Sadly, because of how violent TV and video games are becoming, your child's symptoms could get worse. By promoting exercise and sleep, patients frequently have a lot of energy. Organized sports and other physical activities can assist them in focusing their attention on particular movements and skills while also letting them release their energy in healthy ways. To reduce activity for about an hour before bedtime, set aside a buffer period. Try coloring, reading, or other quiet games to pass the time.

Hug your child for ten minutes. In addition to offering a chance to unwind, this will foster a feeling of love and security. Fill your child's room with lavender or other scented candles. Your child might feel more at ease thanks to the scent.

To help your child drift off to sleep, play soothing tapes in the background. Nature is just one of the many available variations

Teach Your Children How to Socialize

Simple social interactions can be difficult for kids with Adhd. They might find it difficult to read social cues, talk too much, make too many interruptions, or come off as aggressive or "too intense." Because of their comparatively immature emotional development, they may stand out from peers their age and become the target of cruel teasing.

Offer Kudos and Support

Praise should be used to encourage good behavior. Both teaching them what behaviors are acceptable and teaching them what behaviors are unacceptable are crucial for ADHD children.

Instead of just saying "Thanks for doing that," make specific compliments like, "You washed the dishes well. I appreciate you.
.

Minimize your Distractions

It is beneficial to keep a child's environment clear if they are easily distracted. Radios and televisions could be turned down or off based on the child's preferences.

Toys should be put away when they are working on something in their bedroom and getting them to work on tasks away from the allure of TVs or games is crucial.

Instead of Ordering Explain

Where it is age-appropriate for the child, a parent may explain the request. Maintain simplicity but be prepared to be asked to elaborate.

An ADHD child's anxiety and confusion can be reduced by explaining the purposes of a task. A person should use reassuring language when explaining things.

Respectful parenting also entails explaining to the child why they are being asked to perform a task, as self-respect is essential if the child feels different from other children.

Do not become Overburdened

When a parent is overly stressed, not only does their well-being suffer, but they may also be less effective at supporting their child.

Asking for assistance can be helpful if one's workload and obligations become too much.

Don't Speak Negatively

A child with ADHD may feel that they are disliked or that they always do things wrong.

Reinforcing this with negative language can be hurtful and exacerbate disruptive behaviors. Positive feedback can help build a child's confidence. Parents must find a way to voice their worries because it is impossible to always be optimistic. This could be a friend, spouse, or therapist.

Specify a Structure

A daily schedule can give structure and help prevent unplanned interruptions. For kids with ADHD, knowing what to expect can be calming. It may also be an effective way to teach children about responsibility.

Social Circumstances

Keep social interactions brief and to the point. Invite friends over, but limit playtimes to prevent your child from losing self-control. Avoid trying to do this when your child is hungry or tired, like after a day at school.

Get Involved Right Away

Keep an eye out for cautionary signs. Intervene if your child appears to be growing irritable, overexcited, or about to lose control. If at all possible, distract your child by removing them from the situation. This might make them feel better.

Additionally, it's critical to keep in mind that kids with ADHD possess strengths and admirable qualities that deserve to be praised. Being more vivacious is one of their strengths and can be useful in both personal and professional situations.

Recognize your child's strengths, debunk myths, and assist them in obtaining the accommodations they require to improve their quality of life. This will help create a setting for them to succeed, along with your love and support.

Methods for Helping ADHD Children Focus

Children with ADHD struggle significantly with focus and attention. Those youngsters frequently lose focus, jump from one activity to another, and disregard the rules. It can be difficult for parents to discipline their children or get them to listen to them, complete their homework, or clean up after themselves. When educating their children about focus and concentration, parents of children with ADHD must be innovative.

Move Around

Little ones enjoy being active and running around. Throwing a ball back and forth can help you concentrate better. Give your child directions as you throw the ball to them. You can advise him or her to complete a specific task on a specific day or to go to bed at a specific time. Each time your child throws the ball, ask them to repeat the instructions to you. By using this method, the instruction is connected to an enjoyable, visual, and kinesthetic memory, which might aid in aiding retention.

Stop Moving and Pay Attention.

There are always opportunities to help your child focus, and one of the best times to do so is when they least expect it. "Freeze and focus" is a helpful technique. The game's rules are that you can ask your child to "Freeze and focus" at any time. He or she will now remain motionless (freeze) and silent for 5 to 10 seconds. Ask your child to list two or three things they observed or heard while being "frozen" after the allotted time has passed. By saying, "Freeze!" and using the "focus" time to finish these tasks, you can modify the game in the future to include activities you would like your child to complete, such as chores.

Employ Music

The use of music may be an excellent way to reinforce rules, offer directions, or aid with spelling, as well as assist children to remember things. Your youngster can spell a word as you make up a melody for it, or you can sing a home rule. Pick out or compose a special song that your youngster may sing while engaging in especially unpleasant tasks, like cleaning the dishes. It is a simple strategy for enhancing optimism and focus.

Children love doing puzzles, and they are good for developing their fine motor and focus abilities. Word games and logic puzzles are only two of the many different types of puzzles. Make an elaborate treasure hunt with a sequence of deductively logical clues. Allow your child to select a puzzle they enjoy and work on it together to help your child develop concentration and motor skills.

Construct a Novel or a Screenplay

Here's an entertaining exercise to hone your storytelling abilities: As the main character in a novel or movie, ask your youngster to narrate the day. Ask your kid to describe the situation and describe what people did. If there was anything particularly thrilling or discouraging, ask him or her to describe how he or she felt in those instances. Even if it was just a typical day, make sharing stories a habit. If you do this regularly, your child will start to internalize his or her daily routine and view it favorably.

Chapter 4

The Positive Side of ADHD

You start to worry when your child is identified as having attention-deficit/hyperactivity disorder (ADHD). What will other parents and kids think of my child? Will my child be successful in school and find a fulfilling career? Even though children with ADHD undoubtedly face difficulties, it's important to acknowledge and discuss with your child the positive aspects of ADHD.

Some personal strengths can turn to have ADHD into a benefit rather than a disadvantage. Not everyone with ADHD has the same personality traits. A diagnosis of ADHD does not necessarily mean that a person will be at a disadvantage in life. On the contrary, it can and has helped many performers, athletes, and businesspeople succeed. There are numerous examples of people with ADHD who have excelled in their fields.

The good news is that ADHD children can learn to funnel and improve their positive traits, strengths, and talents to help them lead a fulfilled life. If your child has been diagnosed with ADHD, you shouldn't be disheartened or let the condition's many potential advantages overshadow its many disadvantages. Their many, incredible, and in the end valuable strengths are a great asset. These are a few of them:

Energy

Some people with ADHD frequently possess seemingly limitless amounts of energy that they can direct toward achievement on the playing field, in the classroom. The energy and ambition of children with ADHD can be unrestrained when they are given a project or mission they are passionate about. They may become excellent problem-solvers and creative thinkers as a result.

Being Impulsive

Some ADHD sufferers can transform impulsivity into spontaneity. They might be the center of attention or they might be more open to trying new things and bucking the trend. Although it can occasionally be characterized by impulsivity, impatience, and interruptions of others, it can also have benefits. Effectively handling and channeling this symptom can make a person spontaneous, vivacious, and receptive to new experiences. Striking a balance between being overly aroused and bored is a challenge for people with ADHD. Many people find that spontaneous actions keep things interesting and free from other distractions, resulting in enjoyable experiences. This openness to the unexpected could encourage people to follow their passions and put their attention on activities that truly make them happy.

Being Innovative and Imaginative

People with ADHD are frequently very creative, especially when given a task with clear objectives. Due to their intense creativity and willingness to take on tasks that seem impossible, some people with ADHD have been labeled as futurists. People who have ADHD must also approach tasks differently as a result of their condition, making them excellent problem solvers. Due to their unique perspectives, people with ADHD frequently come up with unusual solutions. The person may view life differently as a result of having ADHD, and this may inspire them to approach tasks and situations thoughtfully. As a result, some people with ADHD may have creative minds. They can also be described as original, artistic, and creative.

Utilize the Creative Potential of Your Adhd Child

Here are some suggestions for developing and encouraging your kid's creativity:

1) Dancing and singing
2) Music Performance
3) Establishing and Creating
4)sculpture
5) Sorting and Resolving (mathematics, patterns)
6) Coding (computing) (computing)

Charisma

People with ADHD frequently have a lot of personalities, which makes them not only entertaining to be around but also excellent at igniting others' enthusiasm.

Hyper focusing

The person can perform better by hyper-focusing, which makes them even more productive. They can finish a task this way without being interrupted, and the results are frequently of excellent quality. This causes them to become so totally absorbed in a task that they might not even be aware of their surroundings. This has the advantage of allowing a person with ADHD to focus on a task until it is finished when given one without having to take breaks. A person with ADHD may require assistance at times to use these traits to their advantage.

Examples of Hyperfocus and Its Advantages:

Your child might give all of their focus to schoolwork. Children can excel at anything with dedication and practice, whether it's sports, video games, or musical instruments. By reading, you can help your child become more adept at comprehension and reading by introducing them to a genre they enjoy.
Finding a passion for something that might help them advance in their academic, professional, or professional career.

People with ADHD are frequently excellent conversationalists who speak to their humanity. People with ADHD are frequently talkative, so they can start an interesting conversation in most situations. Higher levels of social intelligence, humor, and empathy may be present in Adhd patients. People with ADHD are particularly adept at enjoying the unexpected events and adventures that keep life interesting.

They are good at improvising because they think quickly and look for quick fixes to problems that arise frequently.

They work tirelessly to get the most out of their interests and delve headfirst into projects that catch their attention.

They are observant and inquisitive, and as a result, they can approach a problem from various angles and offer novel and inventive solutions.

Empathy

A lot of kids with ADHD show a lot of empathy for other people and can comprehend different points of view. Due to this, they make wonderful friends and companions.

Everyone enjoys a good laugh, and children with ADHD are no exception. Children with ADHD not only enjoy a good laugh but frequently have a contagious sense of humor, which makes them enjoyable to be around.

Resilience

Children with ADHD like other "different" children, learn early how to overcome obstacles and deal with criticism. With the right kind of support, people can grow from their missteps, accept one another for who they are, and overcome adversity. In addition, they can assist others in realizing that our differences are what makes us so powerful.

Amazing Problem-Solving Ability

They frequently have exceptional problem-solving abilities. If they become fixated on a difficult challenge, they may overreact in trying to solve it, in addition to the possibility that the situation will grow tedious to them once it is no longer a challenge. They occasionally tend to offer a straightforward yet efficient solution to a conundrum or issue that might stump someone with an average IQ.

While your child may already possess all of these admirable qualities, they might need additional support to mature fully. Children with ADHD can learn to channel their energy in productive ways and advocate for themselves to have their needs met by attending specialized ADHD summer camps. Your child can learn to develop their talents, get better at difficult things, and increase self-esteem with the aid of ADHD specialists.

The fact that your child has Adhd is just one aspect of who they are, but it has the potential to be very beneficial. Maintaining focus on your child's many strengths will help you and those around you start to see them through a new lens rather than focusing solely on their difficulties.

Chapter 5

How can ADHD Kids Be Focused In School and How Teachers Can Help

It can be difficult to manage students with ADHD who are impulsive, hyperactive, and unfocused. You know they have the ability, but they just don't seem to be able to focus on what you are trying to tell them. They disrupt the entire class, which detracts from the learning process.

Individuals with Adhd may:

- By speaking out of turn or circling the room, you might draw attention to yourself.
- Having problems with operations that call for ordered steps, such as lengthy division or calculating equations. This is especially true when instructions are provided in a list.

- Homework assignments are frequently not written down, not finished, or not brought to school.
- Lack of fine motor control makes it difficult to take notes and difficult to decipher handwriting.
- Have issues with lengthy undertakings that lack direct supervision, do not do their share of the job when in a group and could even prevent a group from finishing a task.

Consider the things that kids must complete in the classroom: Become still, adhere to advice, and concentrate. Children with attention deficit hyperactivity disorder (ADHD) struggle to accomplish these very things; it's not that they don't want to; it's just that their brains aren't wired to allow it. That doesn't make teaching them any simpler.

Low grades, scolding and punishment, peer taunting, and low self-esteem are common consequences of ADHD in children. While this is going on, the teacher feels bad because you can't help the child with ADHD and have to deal with concerns from parents who think their children are being mistreated in class. It doesn't have to be this way. There are techniques you may use to support children with ADHD in the classroom, assist them to overcome their learning difficulties and keep their attention without distracting others

How Teachers Can Assist Children With ADHD

So how can you instruct a child that isn't willing to sit down and listen? With a great deal of perseverance, imagination, and reliability, It is your responsibility as a teacher to assess each student's unique requirements and abilities. When you have techniques in place, you can assist children with ADHD to concentrate, remain on target, and learn as much as they are capable of.

The following three elements are incorporated into effective programs for children with ADHD:

What you can do to facilitate learning for students with Adhd

Accommodations.

Instruction: the techniques you employ when instructing.

Intervention: The process you use to stop actions that disturb focus or occupy other pupils.

However, a positive outlook is your most powerful weapon in aiding a student with ADHD. Offer to engage with the student as a partner to "find out solutions together to assist you to get your job done." Reassure the student that you will be watching for appropriate conduct and high-caliber work, and specify when. Additionally, make an effort to overlook inadvertent, somewhat improper behavior that doesn't distract or disturb the less important activities.

Seating

The ADHD student should be seated away from the door and any windows. Students who are seated in rows, facing the teacher, perform better than those who are seated at tables or in other places where they are facing one another.

Establish a distraction-free space where you can concentrate on studying and taking tests. One at a time, repeat instructions as necessary. Work on the hardest material first thing in the morning, if you can.

- Use visuals such as charts, images, and color coding.
- Make note-taking outlines that organize the information as you deliver it.
- Reduce the number of items on worksheets and tests, administer short quizzes frequently in place of lengthy exams, and administer fewer timed exams.

ADHD students should be tested in the formats that work best for them, such as filling in the blanks or orally.

Set a deadline for the completion of each segment of a long-term project.

When giving out assignments, ask three different students to repeat them. After that, have the entire class say the assignment aloud and write it on the board.

Although children with Adhd are capable of thriving in the classroom, getting them there frequently necessitates careful preparation and collaborative work. You might be curious as to how your kid can be academically successful while also being mentally, physically, and emotionally capable. Set up your kid for academic success by utilizing these methods.

Keep Expectations Consistent

Classroom rules should be clear and concise. Rules and expectations for the class should be regularly reviewed and updated when necessary. Rules should be posted in the classroom where they can be easily read. To make sure they comprehend rules, expectations or other instructions, having a child repeat them back is frequently helpful. The possibility that a child heard what was said but misunderstood what it meant should be considered by teachers. A schedule that is readily available and frequently reviewed can help transitions for kids who have trouble managing their time and "shifting gears" from one task or class to the next. Another option for letting a student know how much time is left for an activity is to use timers, taped time signals, or verbal cues.

Decrease Distractions

Due to their susceptibility to distractions, students with ADHD may benefit from being seated away from potential sources of disruption in the classroom, such as doors, windows, and cubby spaces. As much as you can, try to keep the room free of additional distractions like loud music or distracting visuals like clutter. Being seated near the front of the class, close to the teacher, may be beneficial if a child has a particularly hard time managing distractions. While some children with ADHD find listening to "white noise" or relaxing background music to be helpful, it can be distracting for those who do not.

Give Regular Feedback

Feedback on behavior that is frequent and immediate is beneficial for both children with and without ADHD. Any penalties imposed for inappropriate behavior should be given as soon as possible, if necessary.

Reward Good Conduct

When trying to motivate a student, rewards and incentives should always come first.

Change up the rewards frequently. Physical activity helps children with ADHD and may help them focus more clearly after being outside or in gym class. For children with ADHD, a school should continue to feel like a positive environment, so rewards over punishment should take precedence.

Allow them a break

Giving children with ADHD frequent opportunities to stand up and move around can be extremely beneficial because these children frequently struggle with sitting still for extended periods. You can give them a physical break by having them distribute or gather papers or classroom supplies, run errands to the office or other parts of the building, or erase the board. Allowing them to go get a drink of water can be as simple as giving them a brief period of activity.

Utilize instruments and flexible rules

Students with ADHD often have restless personalities. While it's customary for students to sit in their seats during lessons, allowing a child with ADHD to stand up might help them focus better.

The efficacy of prayer in these circumstances should not be undervalued, to sum up. Praying helps you be a better parent and teacher when combined with knowledge from science and medical professionals. There is hope whether you are just beginning to research childhood ADHD or your child has already been diagnosed. Learn more, pay attention, and trust in God. Encourage yourself by remembering that God made your child precisely who He intended. It doesn't matter if they have Adhd that reality will be beautiful.